THE BUSHEY ACADEMY
LRC
LONDON ROAD
BUSHEY WD23 3AA
Tel: 0208 950 9502

CHERRYTREE BOOKS

THE LIVING PLANET
VOLCANOES

Edited by Tom Mariner

LEARNING RESOURCE CENTRE
BUSHEY HALL SCHOOL
LONDON ROAD, BUSHEY
HERTS WD2 3AB

A Cherrytree Book

Adapted by A S Publishing from
Los Volcanes © Parramon Ediciones S.A. 1996
Text: Nuria Roca, Marta Serrano
Illustrations: Miquel Ferron
Design: Beatriz Seoane

This edition first published in 1997
by Cherrytree Press Ltd
a subsidiary of
The Chivers Company Ltd
Windsor Bridge Road
Bath BA2 3AX

© Cherrytree Press Ltd 1997

British Library Cataloguing in Publication Data
Volcanoes. – (The living planet)
1. Volcanoes – Juvenile literature
I. Mariner, Tom
551.2'1

ISBN 0 7451 5317 8

Typeset by Dorchester Typesetting Group Ltd, Dorset
Printed in Spain

All rights reserved. No part of this publication may be reproduced, stored in a retrieval system, or transmitted, in any form or by any means, without the prior permission in writing of the publisher, nor be otherwise circulated in any form of binding or cover other than that in which it is published and without a similar condition including this condition being imposed on the subsequent purchaser.

Dust from the eruption of Mount Pinatubo in the Philippines in June 1991 spread over the whole world.

Contents

The restless earth	4	Famous eruptions	20
Mountains of fire	6	What volcanoes give us	22
Fire down below	8	Forecasting eruptions	24
Types of eruption	10	Volcanoes on other worlds	26
More eruptions	12	Playing with fire	28
Sleeping volcanoes	14	Glossary	30
Rocks from fire	16	Index	32
Flows of lava, ash and mud	18		

VOLCANOES

THE RESTLESS EARTH

VOLCANOES ARE not scattered at random over the earth's surface. Most of them occur in easily recognisable chains, or belts. A German scientist, Alfred Wegener, produced an explanation of this curious fact earlier this century, but not until the 1960s did his idea of continental drift become fully accepted. Wegener argued that today's continents once formed a single landmass, which he named Pangaea.

Wegener maintained that Pangaea broke up into pieces that drifted centimetre by centimetre over millions of years until they arrived where they are now. Movement was possible because about 100 kilometres down in the earth the rocks are partly molten and act as a paste-like liquid on which the continents float. This substance is called magma and the currents that flow in it are the forces that move the continents about.

300 million years ago

200 million years ago

60 million years ago

Now

It is now believed that the outer layers of the earth, beneath the oceans as well as the continents, are divided into huge slabs called plates. The crust is weakened where two plates collide or rub against each other and it is along jagged boundaries that volcanoes are found. On the ocean floor magma wells up where plates are moving apart. It cools and forms new crust, causing the ocean floor to spread.

1. Crust
2. Mantle
3. Outer core
4. Inner core

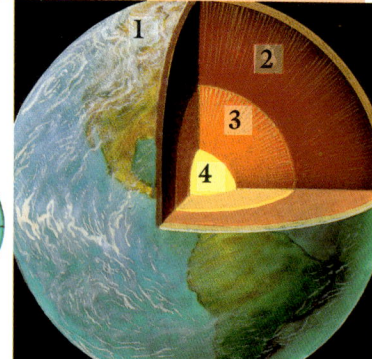

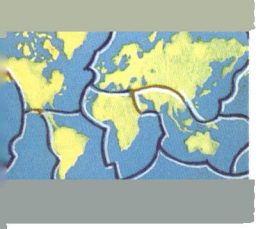

The super continent Pangaea existed about 180 million years ago. Weaknesses in the earth's crust caused it to split into several pieces which drifted slowly over the earth's surface until they arrived where they are now.

VOLCANOES

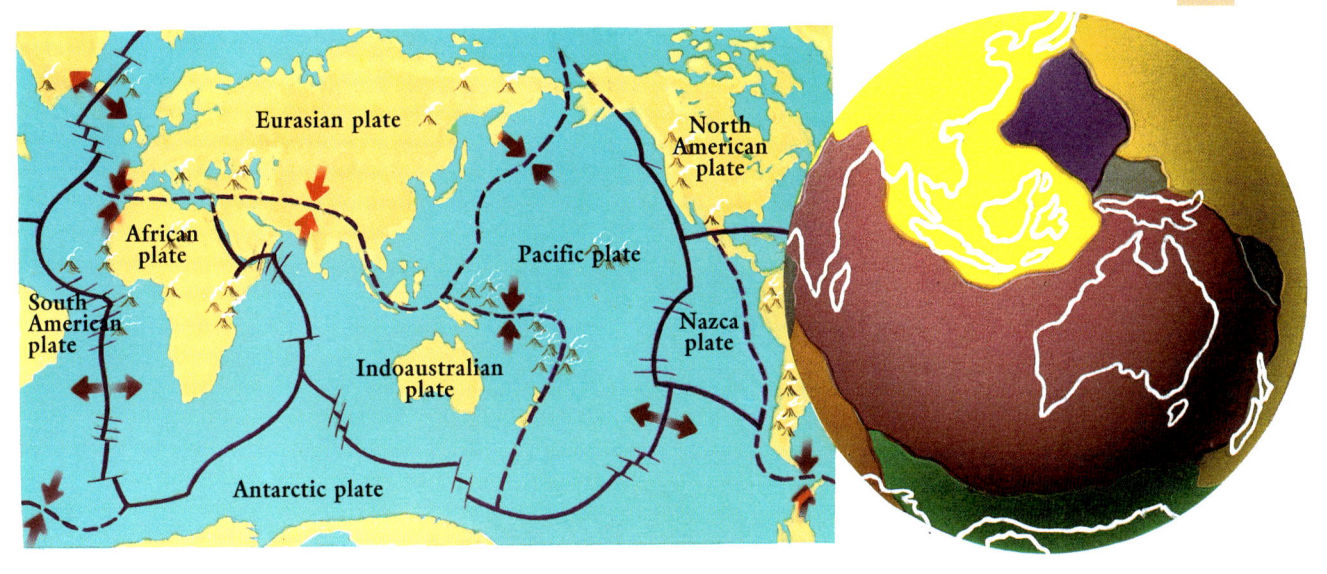

There are eight major plates plus an assortment of smaller ones. They vary between 50 and 100km deep. The map above shows that the plates are capped by both continental and oceanic crust. Currents in the upper mantle beneath shift them around. Most volcanoes are found and most major earthquakes occur around the plate edges.

1. Area of subduction, which creates an oceanic trench and can cause volcanoes.

2. Area of separation, which creates submarine mountain ranges – ocean ridges – and the expansion of the ocean floor.

3. Area of collision, which can cause large chains of mountains.

4. Lateral slipping, which can cause earthquakes.

Arrows on the map show where plates are moving apart and where they are in collision. They indicate that the zones of separation lie under the oceans. Any gap that opens as plates move apart is filled by magma rising from below. This then solidifies on the ocean floor to form ridges of new rock. Where plates meet head-on their edges may buckle and be thrust upwards to form mountain chains. The most spectacular is in northern India where the collision of two plates has created the Himalayas.

Another kind of contact between plates actually destroys the crust. The rock of oceanic plates is heavier than that of continental plates. As a result, when the two collide, the heavier oceanic crust burrows below the lighter continental crust and then melts to become magma below.

Plates that collide or slide one under the other cause volcanic eruptions and earthquakes. The Pacific Ocean crust is disappearing under the lighter crust of the Americas and eastern Asia. The many volcanoes that circle the Pacific are called the Ring of Fire.

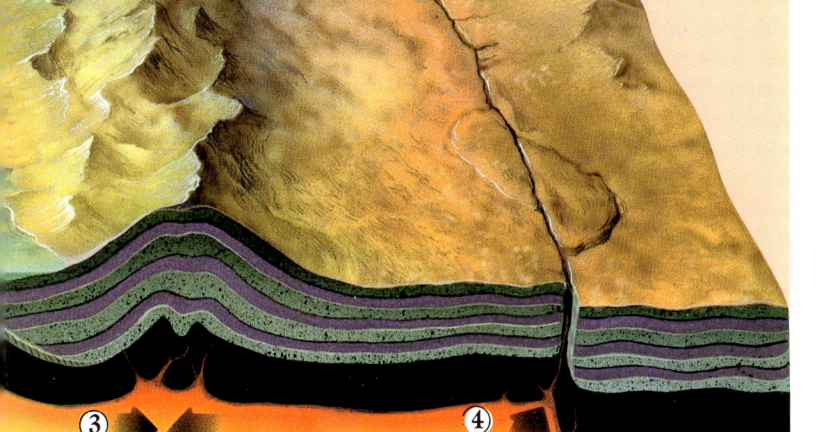

5

VOLCANOES

MOUNTAINS OF FIRE

VOLCANOES ARE named after Vulcano, an Italian island lying north of Sicily. The volcano has been active for thousands of years and the ancient Romans named their god of fire, Vulcan, after it. Vulcan was blacksmith to the gods. The Romans believed that the smoke and fire rising from the volcano came from Vulcan's forge where he and his assistants the Cyclops were at work in his smithy below.

A volcano is a vent or fissure (crack) in the earth's crust through which magma from deep under the earth reaches the surface.

Volcanoes fall into two main groups. Shield volcanoes form from fissures, or cracks, in the earth's crust. Lava pouring from the cracks looks like lines of fire. It spreads over the land and successive flows build up into a gently sloping dome, like an upturned saucer.

Central volcanoes mostly emit lava and ash through one main hole, or vent, called a crater. Far below the surface lies a huge chamber of magma. The magma is full of gas under immense pressure. A duct called a chimney leads from the chamber to the crater at the surface. When the volcano erupts, the pressure in the chamber forces the gas and molten magma upwards through the chimney to emerge through the crater. Magma becomes lava once it has reached the surface where it cools and solidifies round the crater. In time it becomes a cone-shaped mountain.

6

VOLCANOES

An active volcano is one that is known to have erupted at least once in historic times. When an active volcano is not erupting it is dormant. A volcano is called extinct when it is not expected to erupt again. Sometimes when a volcano has ceased to erupt, the old crater fills with rain water and forms a lake called a caldera.

There are about 1300 volcanoes scattered throughout the world. Japan alone has over 200. Around the earth some 500 are active and of those around 50 erupt each year. Some are more active than others. Stromboli, a volcano in Italy, is in a state of almost continuous eruption while nearby Vulcanello has not erupted for over a thousand years and may never erupt again.

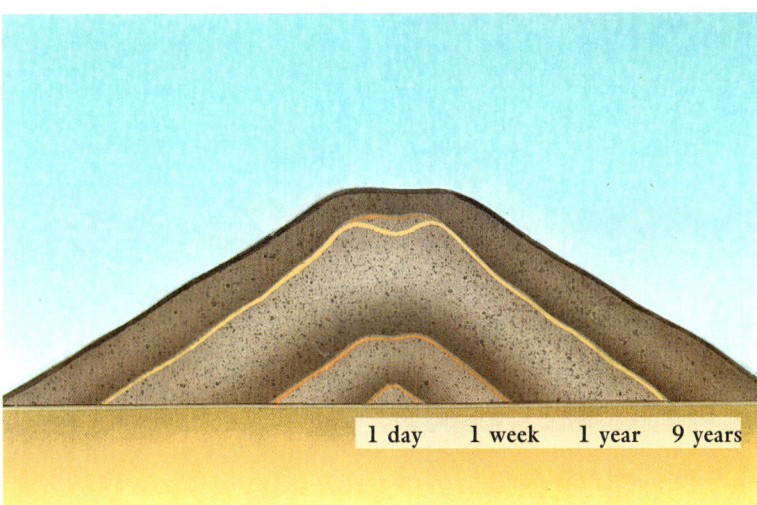

In Mexico in 1943 the appearance of a new volcano gave vulcanologists the chance to study the different phases of a volcano's life telescoped into a period of nine years. The volcano, given the name Paricutín, first appeared without warning as a small mound in a field. After a week the mound had grown to a hill 150m high and within a year it had reached a height of 500m.

No two volcanoes behave in exactly the same way. In general there are active phases during which most of the volcanic activity occurs. There are dormant phases between eruptions and finally extinction.

7

VOLCANOES

Fire down Below

WHEN YOU OPEN a bottle of champagne, unless you are very careful, the pressure of the gas in the bottle forces the wine to spurt out in a sticky cascade. This is exactly what happens, but on a vast scale and with colossal violence when a volcano erupts.

Magma, heated to a temperature of over 1000°C lies in its chamber many kilometres below the crater. Like the champagne, the magma has gas dissolved in it. The volcanic gas is a combination of different substances – mainly superheated steam, carbon dioxide and sulphuric acid. Both the champagne and the magma can hold dissolved gas because both are under pressure, the champagne in its bottle and the magma deep underground. (The pressure at 40km below the earth's surface is nearly 10 tonnes per sq cm.) As the magma rises to the surface the pressure falls, allowing the gases dissolved in it to form bubbles. As the pressure decreases further these bubbles expand until they burst, shattering the volcano and throwing out magma, white-hot rock and ash, which pour down the volcano sides preceded by clouds of flaming gases.

When a volcano erupts the magma acts much like champagne in a bottle when the cork is removed. The gases it contains escape into the atmosphere taking the liquid with it.

8

VOLCANOES

An erupting volcano also throws out lumps of solidified lava, in the form of dust, ash and volcanic bombs. These 'pyroclastic materials' are forced out by an explosion or by the gases set free when magma becomes lava. An eruption also discharges fragments of rock from previous eruptions. Solid materials thrown out during an eruption appear from a distance as a dark cloud rising from the crater. They fall like rain on the surrounding land and form a layer on top of the solidified flows of lava. A section through a typical strato-volcano like this would show solidified lava flows alternating with deposits of pyroclastic materials. Such a volcano is known as an intermediate, or composite, volcano.

When a volcano erupts, some of the magma may emerge as lava. Part of the lava is fluid and pours down the slopes below the crater. The rest is solid pyroclastic material.

When magma comes to the surface its gases are given off and it becomes lava. Rivers of lava flow down the slopes of the volcano. If the lava is of the thin, runny kind, the flow may travel as much as 10km from the crater. If the volcano is near the coast the lava may reach the sea.

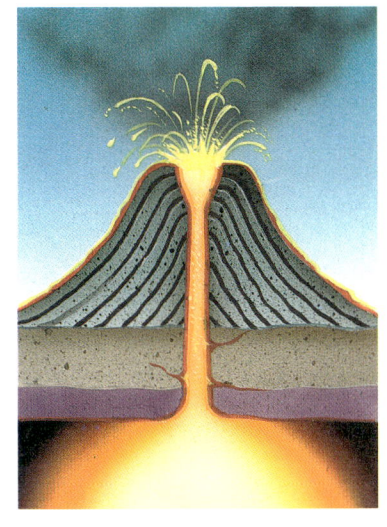

9

VOLCANOES

TYPES OF ERUPTION

WHAT HAPPENS when a volcano erupts depends on the condition of the magma as it pours out over the surface. If the magma is relatively thin and flows easily, the gases it contains escape. Any explosions are usually minor and cause little damage. Thin lava may run down the volcano sides and cover large areas of land round about. Stickier 'viscous' magma moves slowly and tends to cool and solidify at the top of the chimney. If this happens, the magma lower down in the chimney is trapped and forms a blockage inside the volcano. Magma continues to well up from below. Eventually it forces its way through the plug in the throat of the chimney. Immediately the pressure is released the gases in the magma explode. The violence of the explosion depends on how much gas the magma contains.

How a volcano behaves depends on the composition of its magma. Some eruptions are 'quiet' with lava flows but some may be violent if the magma is rich in gas and the chimney is blocked.

Peléean

Hawaiian

Volcanic eruptions fall into several different categories.

HAWAIIAN
The lava is fluid in a Hawaiian eruption and may flow from several vents. It travels swiftly and may flood a wide area, building up a shield volcano. Gases escape easily and little volcanic ash is formed. Kilauea volcano on the island of Hawaii erupts in this way.

VOLCANOES

PELÉEAN
In a Peléean eruption thick, pasty magma solidifies and blocks the chimney. Continued pressure by more rising magma pushes the blockage upwards until it forms a dome above ground. Finally, the pressure that builds up from the gases below is sufficient to split the dome open. A colossal explosion follows, accompanied by huge clouds of white-hot gases, ash and rocks that rush down the volcano's sides. This kind of eruption is named after Mount Pelée, a volcano on the Caribbean island of Martinique. Etna, Europe's largest volcano is of this type.

Strombolian

STROMBOLIAN
The lava in a Strombolian eruption is only moderately fluid and does not form extensive flows. The gases it contains cause fountains of lava to spurt from the crater. The lava solidifies in the air and falls to the ground as round volcanic bombs or as tiny fragments the size of a pea. Strombolian eruptions are named after the volcano Stromboli on an island off the coast of southwest Italy.

Vulcanian

VULCANIAN
In a Vulcanian eruption the lava is very dense and solidifies readily to form a crust in and around the crater. Fresh magma thrusting upwards destroys the crust, turning it into ash which is thrown up as a cloud above the volcano. Vulcanian eruptions are named after Vulcano, the Italian volcano that gave its name to all others.

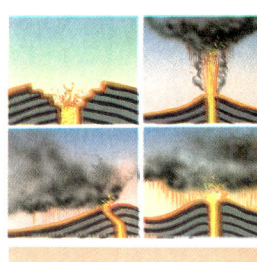

Volcanic eruptions vary from the relatively peaceful Hawaiian type, through Strombolian and Vulcanian to the exceedingly violent Peléean type.

11

VOLCANOES

More Eruptions

NOT ALL ERUPTIONS conform exactly to the four classic types. Fissure eruptions occur when magma escapes along the length of cracks in the earth's crust. These cracks, or fissures, may be many kilometres long. The magma is forced out by the gases dissolved within it. The lava is generally very fluid and may spread out to cover many square kilometres, covering whole regions. Iceland itself is largely composed of lava from eruptions of this type.

Plinian eruptions occur when magma rises through rock saturated with water. The magma turns the water to steam; pressure mounts and produces an explosion. Plinian eruptions are named after Gaius Pliny, a writer of ancient Rome who perished in an eruption of Vesuvius in AD 79.

Icelandic and Plinian eruptions are rare. Icelandic lava flows are gentle but extensive. Plinian eruptions are violent and destructive.

Fissure eruption

Before — Krakatoa

After

The Indonesian island of Krakatoa was blown apart by a Plinian eruption in 1883. There were originally three volcanoes on the island, but the force of the explosions demolished them. There is still volcanic activity but it has mostly disappeared below water level.

VOLCANOES

Submarine eruption

Eruptions that take place deep in the oceans rarely cause explosions because the pressure of the water prevents gas escaping from the magma. The lava solidifies rapidly when it comes into contact with cold ocean water. It forms a thin crust which is fractured as fresh lava rises from below.

In contrast, eruptions that take place in shallower water are often violent since the gases in the magma are able to escape. Jets of superheated steam spurt from the water and clouds of ash hang over the scene. Submarine volcanoes build up cones of ash and rock under water just like those thrown up on dry land. If the tops of these cones appear above the water they form new islands.

Surtsey

A modern example of an island formed by an undersea volcano is the island of Surtsey off the south coast of Iceland. In November 1963 steam jetted out and violent underwater explosions hurled ash and lava bombs high above the water. This activity went on more or less continually for three years. In 1966 lava replaced the steam and ash. It solidified over the new island preventing it from being washed away by the sea.

Submarine eruptions in deep water take place silently and unseen. Eruptions in shallow water may be violent. They pile up cones of volcanic materials which sometimes rise above water to form new islands.

VOLCANOES

Sleeping Volcanoes

Fumaroles are holes in the earth's crust out of which steam and gases pour under pressure. They are found in volcanic areas and the steam is produced by underground magma long after the volcano itself has ceased to erupt.

LONG AFTER a volcano has ceased to cast out molten lava or ashes, minor volcanic activity may continue in the form of fumaroles, hot springs and geysers. Fumaroles are vents through which steam and other gases are given off by a volcano. The vents may be holes in the crater itself or gaps in the sides of the volcano or in the ground nearby. Fumaroles are classified according to their temperature and the gases they give off.

Fumaroles at a temperature of below 200°C that contain gases rich in sulphur are called solfataras, after the dormant volcano Solfatara near Naples in Italy. Solfatara fumaroles are major sources of sulphur used in industry. The salts produced by the acids in the solfatara gases sometimes form deposits of white, yellow, red or clear blue crystals around their vents.

Mofette fumaroles are much cooler. They emit carbon dioxide, oxygen and nitrogen at temperatures of below 90°C. There are numbers of mofettes in Yellowstone National Park in the United States, a region where volcanoes were once active.

VOLCANOES

As molten materials deep in the earth cool down they give off water vapour and carbon dioxide. This hot vapour finds its way upwards through cracks in the rock, cooling as it goes, until it condenses to become water. Finally it gushes from the ground as a hot (thermal) spring. Water from these springs is rich in salts dissolved from the rocks it has passed through on its way to the surface.

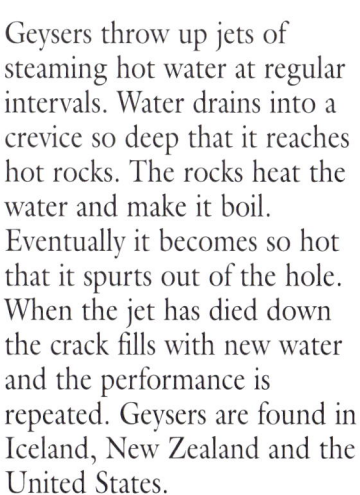

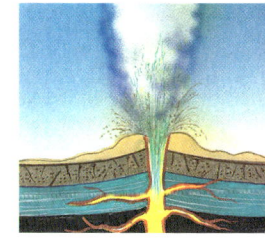

Geysers throw up jets of steaming hot water at regular intervals. Water drains into a crevice so deep that it reaches hot rocks. The rocks heat the water and make it boil. Eventually it becomes so hot that it spurts out of the hole. When the jet has died down the crack fills with new water and the performance is repeated. Geysers are found in Iceland, New Zealand and the United States.

Hot springs occur when water heated in the ground rises and flows out above ground. Geysers spout jets of water and steam often at regular intervals. Hot springs and geysers are rich in mineral salts.

15

VOLCANOES

Rocks from Fire

VOLCANOES ARE not only destructive, they also create new rock. There are two kinds of such rock – pyroclastic and volcanic. Pyroclasts are fragments of lava ejected into the air during an eruption. Volcanic rock is formed when magma from a volcano cools and becomes solid. Both kinds of rock are called igneous, from the Greek word for fire.

Volcanic bomb

Sometimes a volcano flings lava into the air with great force. The lava forms lumps of rock that range in size from tiny particles to bombs more than 30cm in diameter.

PYROCLASTIC ROCKS
Pyroclastic rocks include volcanic bombs made of lava that has partly solidified before it hits the ground. Some weigh as much as 100 tonnes. Large lumps, still molten inside, may become round or egg-shaped in their flight through the air. If the magma is thin and runny and contains little gas it adopts spiral or pear shapes.

When a volcano erupts, old lava from an earlier eruption may be broken into tiny fragments and blasted into the air. These pea-sized fragments are called lapilli.

Ash (made of fragments less than 0.5cm in diameter) and dust (particles less than 0.25mm in diameter) are also cast up during an eruption and mix with the other pyroclasts. When rain falls, the mixture combines to form tuff, a rock hard and durable enough to be used as building material.

Layers of lapilli

Ash cloud from volcano Augustine

VOLCANOES

Basalt columns

VOLCANIC ROCKS

When lava cools it forms extrusive igneous rocks. Basalt, pumice and obsidian are the commonest kinds of rock derived from lava.

Basalt is a smooth, dark rock. It covers vast areas, notably the Deccan plateau in India and the island of Hawaii. Basalt may cool in the form of columns, as in the Giant's Causeway in Northern Ireland.

Pumice is a very light rock like a dry sponge full of air. It is formed when lava bubbling with gas cools and solidifies very rapidly. Rafts of pumice have been seen floating on the sea after an eruption.

Obsidian is a hard, glassy rock that shatters into pieces with naturally sharp edges. Stone Age peoples used fragments of obsidian to make tools and weapons.

The most important volcanic rocks are basalt, pumice and obsidian. Basalt occurs in huge quantities and may cover vast areas. Pumice is a lightweight rock that floats. Obsidian is hard, smooth and glassy.

17

VOLCANOES

Flows of Lava, Ash and Mud

LAVA SOLIDIFIES in a variety of forms. The difference depends on what kind of lava it is, the rate at which it cools, the mixture of gases it contains and the nature of the surface it flows over.

One of these kinds of lava is called by its Hawaiian name aa. It occurs when a sheet of very sticky lava cools very rapidly producing a surface covered with a jumble of jagged blocks.

Ropy, or corded, lava, known also by its Hawaiian name pahoehoe, is formed when lava cools slowly and its gases are given off gradually and gently. The lava solidifies in such a way that it often looks like piles of coiled rope. Even when the upper layers of lava have cooled to form a thick crust of solid rock, hot lava from the volcano continues to flow in tunnels below the surface.

Aa

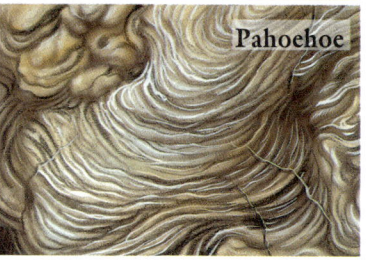

Pahoehoe

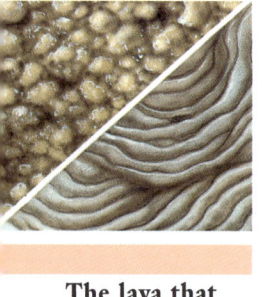

The lava that forms aa rock is thick and sticky. Its name means satiny in Hawaiian. Pahoehoe lava is more runny and solidifies into shapes like coiled rope. Its name means rough or spiny.

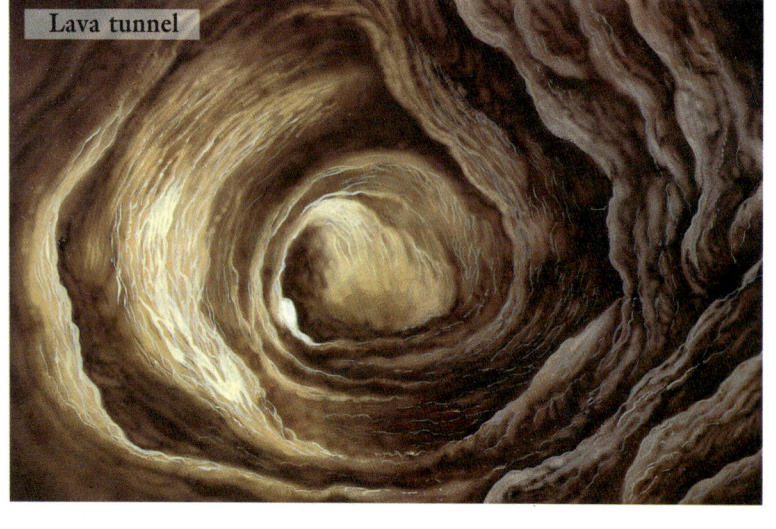

Lava tunnel

Nuée ardente

The most spectacular and destructive volcanic eruptions are those that produce pyroclastic flows and flows of mud. Pyroclastic flows consist of white-hot volcanic ash and dust suspended in flaming gases. Thrown out by the volcano, this terrifying mixture races down the volcano sides. Called a nuée ardente (glowing cloud), it destroys everything in its path. The temperature of pyroclastic flows may be as high as 800°C and they can reach speeds of up to 200km/h.

A recent example of a pyroclastic flow occurred in May 1980 when the volcano of Mount St Helens in the western United States erupted. The explosion blew off the top of the mountain and a fiery avalanche poured down the mountainside. Some 57 people were killed and every tree for miles around was flattened and burnt.

VOLCANOES

Mt St Helens

Pre-1980

The eruption of Mount St Helens in Washington State, USA, in 1980 caused the entire north face of the volcano to collapse. An avalanche of rocks, ice, snow, earth and uprooted trees from the shattered peak slid down the mountainside. The landslide picked up and carried down enough soil, rock and other materials to bury the surrounding areas in a layer 45m deep.

Volcanic mud flows are capable of travelling long distances. On particularly steep slopes, mud flows have been known to reach speeds of 40km/h. They can be highly dangerous, too. In 1985 the volcano Nevado del Ruiz in Colombia erupted. Ruiz is 5431m high and its summit is covered in snow and ice. In the course of a fairly moderate eruption, great quantities of hot lava and ash from the volcano fell on to the mountain's frozen covering and melted it. Torrents of water poured down the mountainside, washing off the mountain soil as it went. The mixture of water and soil became an avalanche of steaming mud which continued on its downward path until, two hours later, it surprised and overwhelmed the city of Armero and killed 22,000 of its inhabitants.

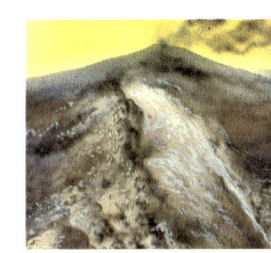

Nevado del Ruiz

Hot lava and ash from an erupting volcano may melt snow and ice lying on its upper slopes. Torrents of water then pour down the mountainside with growing force as they pick up soil and vegetation in their path.

Famous Eruptions

THE WORLD'S MOST closely studied volcano is Kilauea on the island of Hawaii. Modern eruptions on Kilauea are gentle. They are not dangerous so scientists are able to study the volcano at close quarters. In the past 100,000 years Kilauea has grown from sea level to a height of 1247m. The lava is almost free of gas and so thin that it flows like cream.

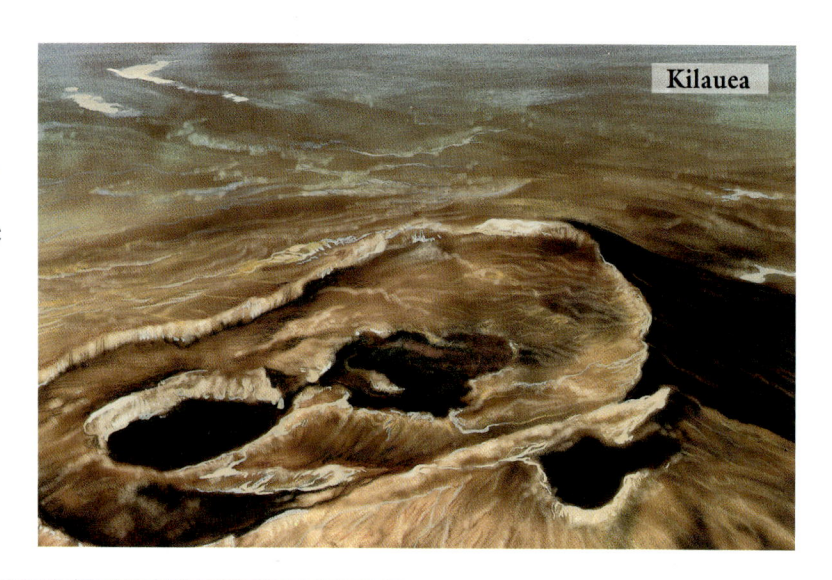

Vesuvius has a history of catastrophic eruptions going back almost 2000 years. By contrast the Hawaiian volcano of Kilauea has been quietly erupting for a long time and geologists have been able to study it at close quarters over many years.

Pliny the Younger wrote the earliest known account of a volcanic eruption. It was in AD 79, the volcano was Vesuvius and the eruption killed his uncle the writer and scientist Gaius Pliny.

Vesuvius had been dormant for a thousand years when it suddenly erupted without warning. The nearby cities of Pompeii and Herculaneum were overwhelmed by a rain of white-hot ashes and mud flows. The two cities and their inhabitants were buried several metres deep and remained hidden until they were revealed by chance in 1709.

There were isolated eruptions during the 1500 years after AD 79, but since a violent eruption in 1631 Vesuvius has been quite active. The last major eruption took place in 1944 when the towns of Massa and San Sebastian were obliterated.

VOLCANOES

Mt Pelée — Before / After

Area affected — Mt Pelée, St Pierre, Martinique

Sumatra, Borneo, Area covered by ash, Krakatoa, Java

Krakatoa — Before / After

In May 1902, the volcano Mount Pelée on the Caribbean island of Martinique began to stir. After several minor eruptions there was a massive explosion and a mighty avalanche of burning ash and boiling lava spewed from the volcano. It raced down the mountain and fell upon the island's capital, St Pierre. Only one of the city's 30,000 people survived. He was a convicted murderer awaiting execution.

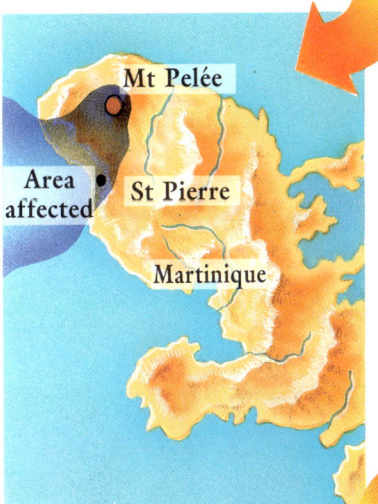

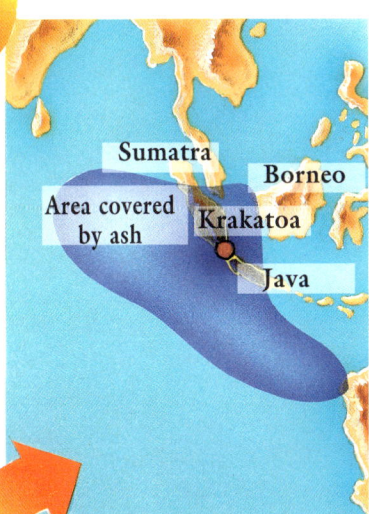

A small uninhabited island once lay in the Sunda Strait between Java and Sumatra. Its name was Krakatoa. In August 1883, after three months of sporadic eruptions from its three volcanoes, a series of colossal explosions blew the island apart. A column of gas and dust 80km high formed over the remains of Krakatoa and ash and pumice fell like rain over an area of 770,000 sq km. The explosion set up tsunamis, gigantic tidal waves, one 40m high, that overwhelmed the shores of neighbouring islands causing widespread damage and killing tens of thousands of people. The sound of the explosion was heard distinctly up to 3000km away. It was the loudest noise of modern times.

In 1883 huge waves created by an eruption on the island of Krakatoa crashed on to the shores of Java and Sumatra drowning many thousands of people. In 1902 St Pierre was wiped out by a fiery avalanche that plunged down the slopes of the volcano Mt Pelée.

21

VOLCANOES

WHAT VOLCANOES GIVE US

MAGMA RISING from the earth's interior contains a wealth of chemicals and minerals. As magma solidifies, hot underground water carries these substances away and deposits them in joints and fissures in the rocks. Important among these deposits are gold, silver, mercury, copper, lead, zinc and other metals, minerals and chemicals that are used in industry.

Some deposits, such as sulphur, are brought to the surface around the mouths of hot springs and volcanic vents. Diamonds, the hardest of all natural substances, are produced by underground volcanic activity. They are composed of pure carbon and are formed under enormous pressure in deposits of a rare rock called kimberlite.

Magma is the source of minerals and metals in daily use. Geothermal energy can only be used where it is easy to reach, as in Iceland. Both New Zealand and Italy use underground steam to produce electricity.

Energy obtained from the earth's internal heat is called geothermal energy. Everywhere under the earth, temperature increases with depth. There are, however, few areas where heat from inside the earth can be made use of effectively. Certain conditions are necessary. The heat must be concentrated and be constantly available in rock formations that are easy to reach and exploit. Iceland leads the world in using volcanic hot water for heating. Every building in the capital Reykjavik is heated in this way, as are greenhouses for growing food.

Steam from underground may be harnessed to produce electricity. The first successful geothermal power station was built in 1904 at Lardarello in central Italy. New Zealand followed in 1958 with a power station at Wairakei.

VOLCANOES

Volcanic materials contain many substances that help plant growth. In tropical areas, heat and heavy rainfall take only a few years to turn the lava and ash from an eruption into deep and fertile soil. People living in these areas rely on periodic volcanic eruptions to renew the soil and provide fresh nutrients for their crops to grow.

In some places, extinct craters and basins formed by volcanic action are of great benefit to farmers. Water collects in them and they shelter growing crops from winds. In Mexico, delicate crops that need protection and rich soil are grown in volcanic hollows. On the Canary Islands crops are grown in old craters that provide shelter from the drying effect of the wind. The island of Lanzarote is particularly dry. Farmers there cover the soil in their fields and gardens with layers of pea-sized volcanic rock to shield it from wind and sun to stop it drying out.

Volcanic rock is rich in the minerals that keep plants healthy and help them to grow. As a result, soil in volcanic areas is usually very fertile. Old craters and basins are also used for growing crops.

23

VOLCANOES

Forecasting Eruptions

Because volcanic soil is so fertile, areas around volcanoes are often densely populated. But volcanoes can be dangerous neighbours. In the past 2000 years almost a million people have perished in volcanic eruptions. The deadliest volcanoes are those that have lain dormant for a long time. They give people a false sense of security and when they do erupt they cause huge destruction and loss of life.

Because of the fertility of volcanic soil, volcanic areas are often densely populated, despite the danger of an eruption. Observatories have been set up close to certain volcanoes to study them and warn of possible eruptions.

In some places observatories have been set up near to active volcanoes to study them and try to forecast eruptions. Local historical records give useful evidence, too, since a volcano's past performance may provide clues to its future behaviour. The kinds of deposit laid down by earlier eruptions are also important indicators of how the volcano is likely to behave next time.

Using highly sensitive equipment, the observatory staff keep a constant record of all earthquake activity and of any changes in the level of the land in the neighbourhood. They also make daily checks on the kinds of gases emitted by the volcano and measure the temperature of local fumaroles and of lakes that have collected in the crater since the last eruption.

VOLCANOES

Predicted extent of mud flow at Armero

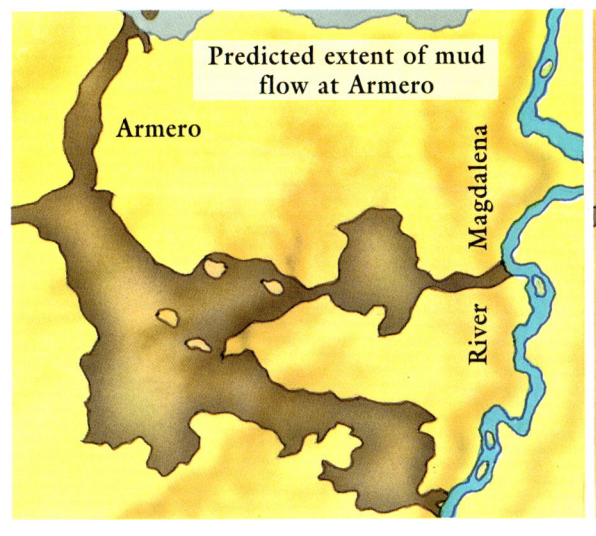

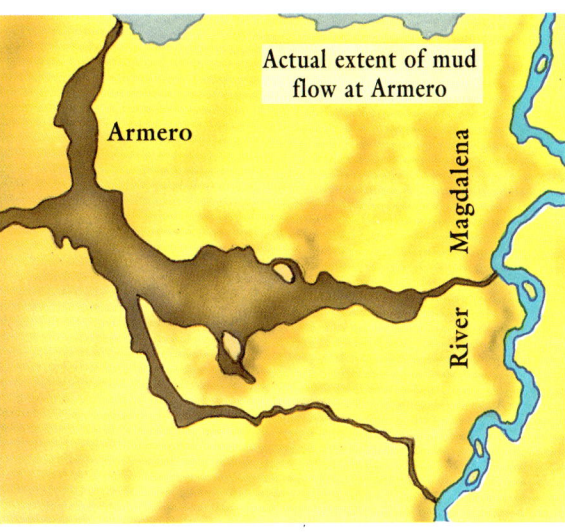

Actual extent of mud flow at Armero

In 1983 the volcano on the tiny Indonesian island of Colo became active. Acting on the advice of watching scientists, the area was evacuated. The entire population fled and a few days later the volcano erupted. Lava flows and a rain of red-hot ash blanketed the island but, thanks to the warning, all the island's 7000 people had moved to safety.

Another eruption was correctly forecast in 1984 at the Colombian town of Armero. When the nearby volcano of Nevado del Ruiz became active scientists warned that Armero was in danger because it lay in the path of an earlier mud flow. Unhappily the advice was ignored. Shortly afterwards the volcano erupted. A great mud flow slid down the mountain blotting out Armero and killing 22,000 people.

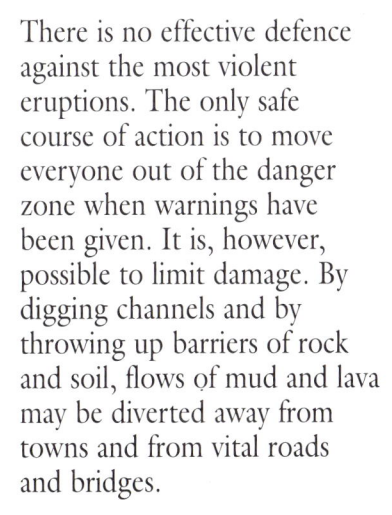

There is no effective defence against the most violent eruptions. The only safe course of action is to move everyone out of the danger zone when warnings have been given. It is, however, possible to limit damage. By digging channels and by throwing up barriers of rock and soil, flows of mud and lava may be diverted away from towns and from vital roads and bridges.

Some volcanic eruptions can now be accurately predicted. Two recent examples were at Colo in Indonesia in 1983 and at Armero in Colombia in 1984.

25

Volcanoes on Other Worlds

Volcanoes and volcanic features are found not only on the earth. There is good evidence of volcanic activity, both past and present, on most of the planets and their satellites in the solar system.

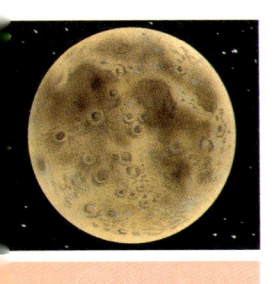

Huge volcanoes and vast lava fields have been observed on the planet Mars. Mars possesses the largest known volcano in the solar system. Mount Olympus is 25km high and 600km across. It could easily swallow up a city the size of London. Olympus seems to be extinct. Its last eruption is thought to have taken place about 200 million years ago.

By observation and from space flights we know that evidence of volcanic activity is widespread throughout the solar system. Mars possesses several enormous volcanoes and much of the moon's surface is covered by ancient lava flows.

Most of the many craters on the moon have been caused by the impact of gigantic meteorites but some other features are the result of the moon's own volcanic activity. What look like seas are in fact huge basins that were flooded with basalt lava three or four billion years ago. The moon's lava must have been very liquid to have covered such huge areas.

VOLCANOES

Venus is the planet nearest to earth but thick clouds hide its surface from sight. Space probes, however, have penetrated the planet's poisonous atmosphere and revealed that many of its surface features are the result of volcanic activity. The orbiting space probe Magellan sent back images in 1990 of craters and other features that one would expect to find in volcanic regions. The dense cloud that envelopes Venus seems also to have volcanic origins since the gases it consists of are typical of volcanic eruptions. Furthermore, lightning has been observed close to volcano-like features on the surface. As on earth, lightning could be triggered by clouds of ash from volcanoes.

Venus is wrapped in thick clouds but space probes have detected volcanic features on its surface. Other space probes reveal that Jupiter's satellite Io is the most volcanically active body we know of in the solar system.

Io, a satellite of Jupiter, is only a little larger than our moon. Nevertheless Io wins first prize for volcanic activity in the solar system. Pictures sent back by the Galileo space probe in 1996 revealed a surface pitted by well over 1000 craters and evidence of recent deposits of volcanic materials. Numbers of volcanoes were erupting and giving off towering clouds of gas and ash that rose some 300km above them.

27

Playing with Fire

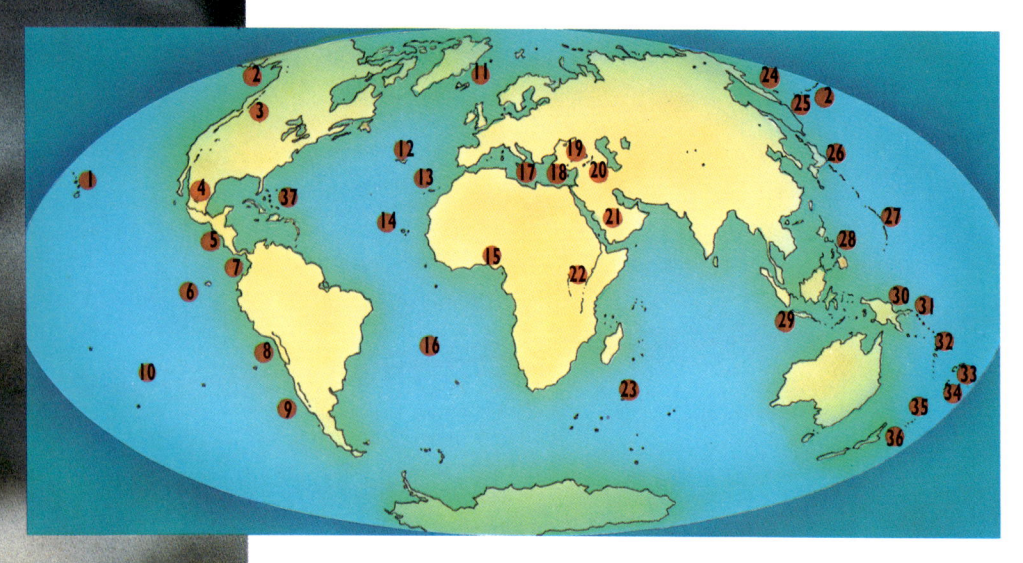

1. Hawaiian Islands	19. Turkey
2. Alaska	20. Iran
3. Cascade Mountains	21. Middle East
4. Mexico	22. East Africa
5. Central America	23. Indian Ocean
6. Galapagos Islands	24. Kamchatka
7. Colombia and Ecuador	25. Kuril Islands
8. Peru and Bolivia	26. Japan
9. Chile	27. Mariana Islands
10. South Pacific	28. Philippine Islands
11. Iceland	29. Indonesia
12. Canary Islands	30. Papua New Guinea
13. Azores	31. Solomon Islands
14. Cape Verde Islands	32. New Hebrides Islands
15. Cameroon	33. Samoa
16. South Atlantic	34. Tongan Islands
17. Italy	35. Kermadec Islands
18. Greece	36. New Zealand
	37. Caribbean

TRACE THE VOLCANOES! Volcanoes occur mostly in groups rather than in isolation. Using the map above and the map below, you can easily demonstrate how closely the distribution of volcanoes follows the pattern of the margins between the principal plates of the earth's crust. The upper map shows where the volcanic zones are. The lower map shows the boundaries of the main crustal plates. On a piece of tracing paper, mark the locations of the volcanic groups on the top map then place it over the bottom map.

RING OF FIRE
Volcanic mountain ranges and islands mark the rim of the Pacific Ocean. So many of these volcanoes are active that collectively they are known as the Pacific Ring of Fire. The Mediterranean also has its share of volcanoes. In both these areas neighbouring slabs of the earth's crust are in collision and one is descending beneath another. The crust is weakened, cracks appear and magma forces its way to the surface to form volcanoes. In the Atlantic Ocean two plates are spreading apart. The magma welling up between them has created a huge underwater mountain range called the Mid-Atlantic Ridge. Iceland is an exposed part of this ridge. Can you see which other islands are part of it?

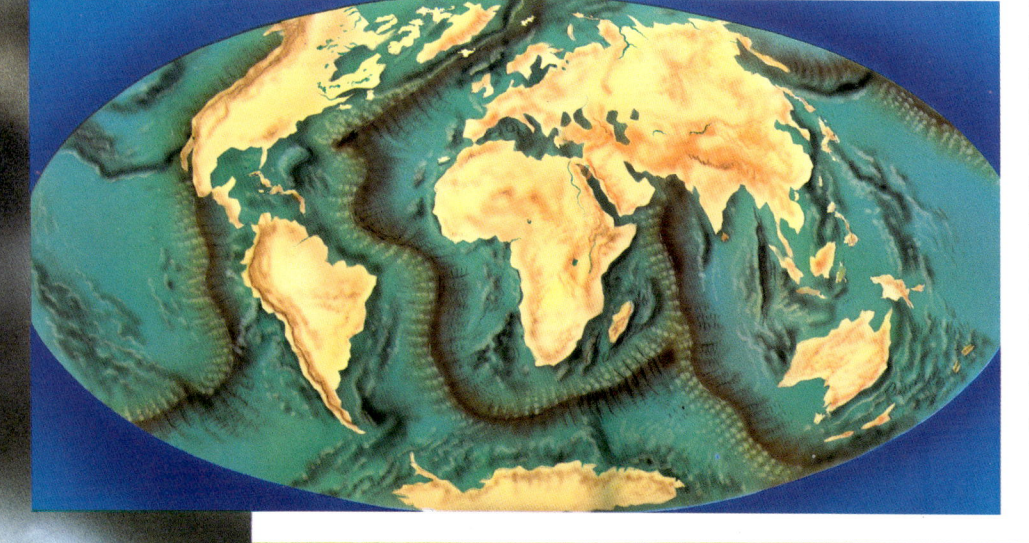

BUILD YOUR OWN VOLCANO
Using a relief map of a volcanic area trace the contours of a volcano and transfer them, one by one and side by side, on to a sheet of cork. The diagram shows you how to do it. With the permission and, if necessary, help of an adult, cut the pieces out and stick them in order, largest at the bottom, smallest at the top. You will have the basic outline of a volcano. Use Plasticene or plaster of Paris to smooth the steps between the contours. Decorate the result according to whether you want the volcano to be erupting, dormant or extinct. If extinct, the volcano would be surrounded by fields of crops, towns and villages.

CONTINENTAL JIGSAW
Once, long ago, there was one giant continent called Pangaea. Pangaea broke up and the pieces drifted apart. See if you can put them back together. Trace the continents (round the continental shelves if you can find a map of them) and carefully cut out the pieces. Try to fit them together to make a single continent.

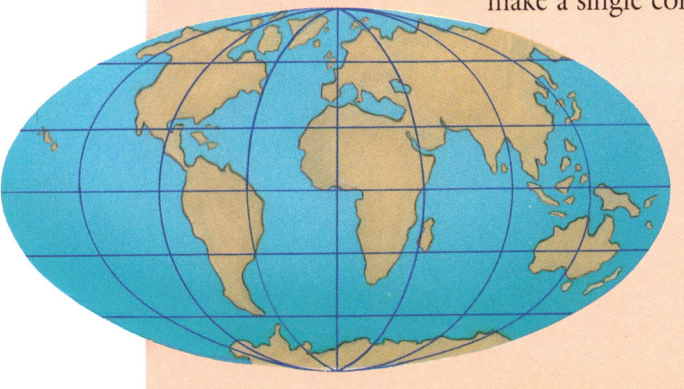

Glossary

AA Hawaiian name for block lava, a type of igneous rock.
ACTIVE VOLCANO Volcano that erupts constantly or occasionally.
ASH Fragments of tephra less than 0.5cm in diameter.
AVALANCHE Mass of rocks (or snow) hurtling down a mountainside.
BASALT Rock formed from solidified lava.
BOMB Large fragment of tephra.
CALDERA Large volcanic crater, sometimes water-filled.
CARBON DIOXIDE One of the gases released during an eruption.
CENTRAL VOLCANO Typical volcano with a reservoir, or chamber, of magma deep under the ground.
CHIMNEY Main channel between the central chamber and the surface created by the pressure or heat of the rising magma.
CONTINENTAL DRIFT Gradual but continuous movement of the great plates that form the earth's crust.
CRATER Central vent of a volcano.
CRUST Thin, rocky, outer layer of the earth.

DORMANT VOLCANO Volcano that has been inactive for too short a time for us to know if it will ever erupt again.
DUST Fragments of tephra less than 0.25mm in diameter.
EXTINCT VOLCANO Volcano that has not erupted in historic times.
FISSURE ERUPTION Type of eruption in which magma bubbles along the length of a crack in the earth's crust.
FUMAROLE Vent that emits gases and steam from a volcano or volcanic region.
GAS Volcanic gas is mostly steam but it looks like smoke because of the dust and ash thrown out with it.
GEOLOGIST Scientist who studies rocks and the earth.
GEOTHERMAL ENERGY Power from underground heat and hot springs.
GEYSER Hot spring that periodically spurts water into the air.
HAWAIIAN Type of eruption that results in shield volcanoes like those on Hawaii.

HOT SPRING Water heated by magma that gushes or seeps from the ground. Also called a thermal spring.
ICELANDIC Type of fissure eruption.
IGNEOUS ROCK Rock formed from solidified magma. Extrusive igneous rocks are formed from magma cooling on the surface. Intrusive igneous rocks are formed from magma that cools below ground.
INTERMEDIATE VOLCANO Volcano whose slopes are built up from layers of ash and lava caused by alternate explosive eruptions and lava spilling quietly from side vents. Sometimes called composite volcanoes.
LAPILLI Pea-sized volcanic bombs.
LAVA Magma that reaches the surface.
MAGMA Molten rock below the earth's surface.

MANTLE Layer of the earth's interior immediately below the crust.
MINERAL Non-living substance made of elements. Different rocks are formed from different minerals.
MOFETTE Type of fumarole that emits gases up to 90°C in temperature.
MUD FLOW Boiling stream of volcanic ash and water.
OBSIDIAN Kind of glassy igneous rock.
PAHOEHOE Hawaiian word for ropy lava, an igneous rock.
PELÉEAN Violent eruption that results from the pressure of gas in sticky magma.
PLATE One of the pieces of earth's outer layers that float like huge rafts on the molten rock below.
PLINIAN Type of explosive eruption that results when magma meets rock saturated with water.
PUMICE Lightweight igneous rock formed from frothy lava.
PYROCLASTIC MATERIAL Dust, ash and larger fragments of lava. Also called tephra.

ROPY LAVA Kind of igneous rock. Also called pahoehoe.
SHIELD VOLCANO Low, broad, dome-shaped volcano formed from lava flowing freely from a vent. Several shield volcanoes may overlap.
SOLAR SYSTEM The sun and its family of planets.
SOLFATARA Type of fumarole that emits sulphur gas up to 200°C in temperature.
STRATO-VOLCANO Volcano built up from tephra that falls round crater during explosive eruptions.
STROMBOLIAN Type of eruption in which gas is given off and forms a cinder cone, or central, volcano.
SUBMARINE VOLCANO Volcano that erupts under the sea and sometimes builds up into an island.
SULPHUR Yellow mineral that forms around hot springs.
SULPHURIC ACID Highly corrosive acid formed from sulphur.
TEPHRA Fragments of pyroclastic material including dust, ash and volcanic bombs.

THERMAL To do with heat.
TIDAL WAVE Great wave caused by the tide, or by an earthquake or volcanic eruption. Also called a tsunami.
TSUNAMI Tidal wave caused by an earthquake or volcano.
TUFF Kind of rock formed from volcanic ash.
VENT Hole in the top or side of a volcano.
VOLCANIC BOMB Large fragment of pyroclastic rock (tephra) ejected during an eruption.
VOLCANIC ROCK Igneous rocks formed from lava.
VULCANIAN Eruption that occurs when gas in the magma chamber blasts out a plug of sticky magma in the vent of a volcano.
VULCANOLOGIST Scientist who studies volcanoes.

INDEX

Aa lava 18, *18*
Active volcanoes 7, *7*
  numbers of 7
Armero (Colombia) destroyed 19, *19*, 25, *25*
Ash 9, 16, *16*
  benefits to farmers 23, *23*
  lightning with 27
Augustine (volcano) *16*
Avalanches, volcanic *see* Mud flows; Pyroclastic flows

Basalt 17, *17*
Bombs, volcanic 9, *9*, 11, 16, *16*

Caldera 7
Canary Islands volcanoes 23, *23*
Carbon dioxide 8, 14, 15
Central volcanoes 6
Chimneys 6
  effect of blockage 10, *10*, 11
Colo eruption 25
Composite volcano 9
Cones (ash/rock) 6
  undersea 13, *13*
Continental drift 4-5, *4-5*
Corded lava 18, *18*
Crust: division of 5, *5*
  formation underwater 4

Diamonds, formation of 22
Dormant volcanoes 7, *7*
  dangers from 24
Ducts *see* Chimneys
Dust 9

Earthquakes, where they occur 5, *5*
Eruptions 10-11, *10-11*, 12-13, *12-13*
  central volcanoes 6
  limiting damage 25
  material thrown out *see* Pyroclastic materials
  new volcanoes 7
  trying to forecast 24-25, *24-25*
  see also Pressure
Etna 11
Extinct volcanoes 7
  benefits to farmers 23, *23*

Fissure eruptions 12, *12*
Fumaroles 14. *14*

Galileo (space probe) 27
Gases, volcanic 8-9, *8*
  and types of lava 18
  central volcanoes 6
  checking emissions 24
  fumarole 14, *14*
  size of explosion and 10
  submarine eruptions 13
  what they are 8, *8*
Geothermal energy 22, *22*
Geysers 15, *15*
Giant's Causeway (Northern Ireland) 17

Hawaiian eruption 10-11, *10*
Herculaneum (Italy) destroyed 20
Himalayas, formation of 5

Hot springs 15, *15*

Iceland: eruptions 12, *12*
  geysers 15
  new island *see* Surtsey
Igneous rocks 16-17, *16-17*
Intermediate volcano 9
Io (satellite) 27
Islands, new 13, *13*
  see also Surtsey

Kilauea 11, 20, *20*
Krakatoa 12, *12*, 21, *21*

Lapilli 16, *16*
  use by farmers 23
Lava 9, *9*, 11
  benefits to farmers 23, *23*
  dense/easily solidified 11
  forms 18, *18*
  rocks derived from 17, *17*
  shield volcanoes 6
  solidified airborne *see* Bombs, volcanic
  solidified submerged 13
  Surtsey 13
  thin 20
Lava bombs 13
Lava flows: speed of 9
  see also Pyroclastic flows
Lava tunnels 18, *18*

Magellan (space probe) 27
Magma: benefits from 22, *22*
  central volcanoes 6
  continental drift and 4, 5, *5*
  eruption through water 12, *12*
  Icelandic eruption 12-13, *12-13*
  making new crust 4, 5
  rock derived from 16, *16*
  sticky/viscous 10, 11
  thin/flows easily 10
  see also Gases, volcanic; Lava
Mars (planet) volcanoes 26, *26*
Massa (Italy) 20
Metals, source of 22, *22*
Mid-Atlantic Ridge 28
Minerals, source of 22, *22*
Mofette fumaroles 14
Moon volcanoes 26
Mount Olympus (Mars) 26
Mount Pelée 11, 21, *21*
Mount Pinatubo eruption *2*
Mount St Helens 18, 19
Mud flows 19, *19*, 25, *25*

Nevado del Ruiz 19, *19*, 25, *25*
Nitrogen 14
Noise, loudest ever heard 21
Nuée ardente 18, *18*

Observatories 24, *24*
Obsidian 17, *17*
Oceans: crust formation 4-5
  eruptions under 13, *13*

Pacific Ocean: crust 5
  see also Ring of Fire

Pahoehoe lava 18, *18*
Pangaea: break-up of 4, *4*
  jigsaw 29, *29*
Paricutín 7
Peléean eruption *10*, 11
People: danger from volcanoes 24-25, *24-25*
  benefit from volcanoes 22-23, *22-23*
Plates: areas of collision 5, *5*
  see also Continental drift; Crust
Plinian eruptions 12, *12*
Pliny, Gaius 12, 20
Pliny the Younger 20
Pompeii (Italy) destroyed 20
Pressure, and eruptions 8, *8*
  fumaroles 14, *14*
Pumice 17, *17*
Pyroclastic flows 18, 21, *21*
  Martian 26
Pyroclasts/Pyroclastic materials 9, *9*, 16, *16*

Ring of Fire *5*, 28
Ropy lava 18, *18*

Salts, source of 14, 15
San Sebastian (Italy) destroyed 20
Shield volcanoes 6, 11
  formation of *12*
Soil, volcanic 23, *23*, 24, *24*
Solfatara fumaroles 14
St Pierre (Martinique) destroyed 21, *21*
Steam, superheated 8, 13
Strato-volcano 9
Strobolian eruption 11, *11*
Stromboli 7, 11
Submarine eruptions 13, *13*
Sulphur, source of 14, 22
Sulphuric acid 8
Surtsey 13, *13*

Temperature: fumaroles 14
  magma 8
  pyroclastic flows 18
  see also Geothermal energy
Thermal springs 15, *15*
Tsunami 21
Tuff 16

Vents 10
  see also Fumaroles
Venus (planet) volcanoes 27, *27*
Vesuvius 12, 20, *20*
Volcanic rocks 16, 17, *17*
Volcanoes: build your own 29
  distribution 4-5, 28, *28*
  types of 6
  see also Active volcanoes; Dormant volcanoes; Extinct volcanoes
Vulcan 6
Vulcanello 7
Vulcanian eruption 11, *11*
Vulcano (island) 6, 11

Water vapour 15
Wegener, Alfred 4

Yellowstone National Park (USA) 14